Soils

Andrea Rivera

abdopublishing.com

Published by Abdo Zoom™, PO Box 398166, Minneapolis, Minnesota 55439. Copyright © 2018 by Abdo Consulting Group, Inc. International copyrights reserved in all countries. No part of this book may be reproduced in any form without written permission from the publisher. Abdo Zoom™ is a trademark and logo of Abdo Consulting Group, Inc.

Printed in the United States of America, North Mankato, Minnesota
022017
092017

**THIS BOOK CONTAINS
RECYCLED MATERIALS**

Cover Photo: Brendan Howard/Shutterstock Images
Interior Photos: Brendan Howard/Shutterstock Images, 1; iStockphoto, 4, 6–7, 9, 13, 17, 18, 19; Bluedog Studio/
Shutterstock Images, 5; Jean Cliclac/iStockphoto, 6; People Images/iStockphoto, 8; Lucky Images/
Shutterstock Images, 10; Steve Cole Images/iStockphoto, 11; Elaine Thompson/AP Images, 12; Shutterstock Images,
14–15; Joanna Stankiewicz-Witek/Shutterstock Images, 21

Editor: Emily Temple
Series Designer: Madeline Berger
Art Direction: Dorothy Toth

Publisher's Cataloging-in-Publication Data
Names: Rivera, Andrea, author.
Title: Soils / by Andrea Rivera.
Description: Minneapolis, MN : Abdo Zoom, 2018. | Series: Rocks and minerals |
    Includes bibliographical references and index.
Identifiers: LCCN 2017930229 | ISBN 9781532120480 (lib. bdg.) |
    ISBN 9781614797593 (ebook) | ISBN 9781614798156 (Read-to-me ebook)
Subjects: LCSH: Soils--Juvenile literature.
Classification: DDC 577--dc23
LC record available at http://lccn.loc.gov/2017930229

Table of Contents

Soil makes up the top layer of Earth. It is made of minerals, air, and water. Soil also contains tiny living creatures.

Plant and animal
remains break down.
They become part of soil, too.

Soil comes in many colors.

It is often black
or brown.

Plants grow in soil. It has **nutrients** that help plants grow.

Water seeps into the soil. This gives plants something to drink.

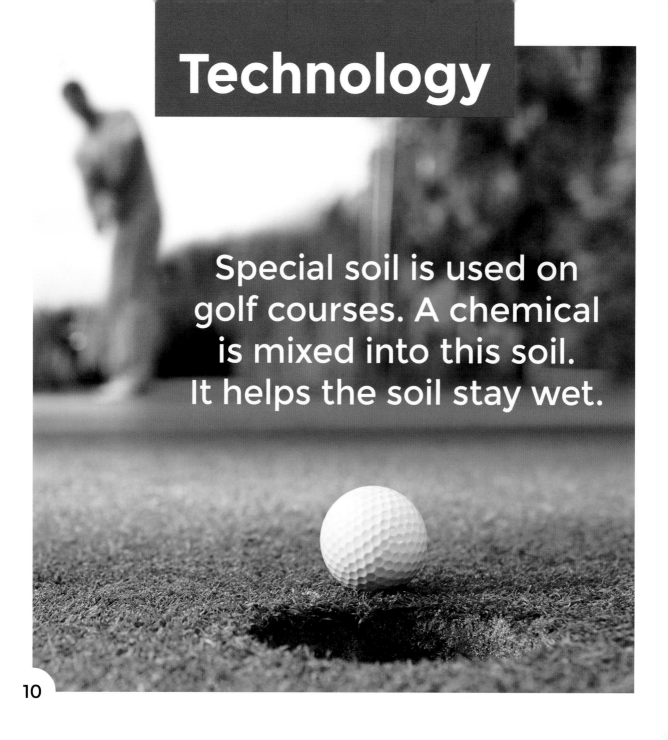

Technology

Special soil is used on golf courses. A chemical is mixed into this soil. It helps the soil stay wet.

The grass on this soil
requires less watering.

Engineering

Rain can turn loose soil into a mudslide. Some areas have many mudslides. Homes in these areas need protection.

Retaining walls help control mudslides. Sandbags help, too. They direct water away.

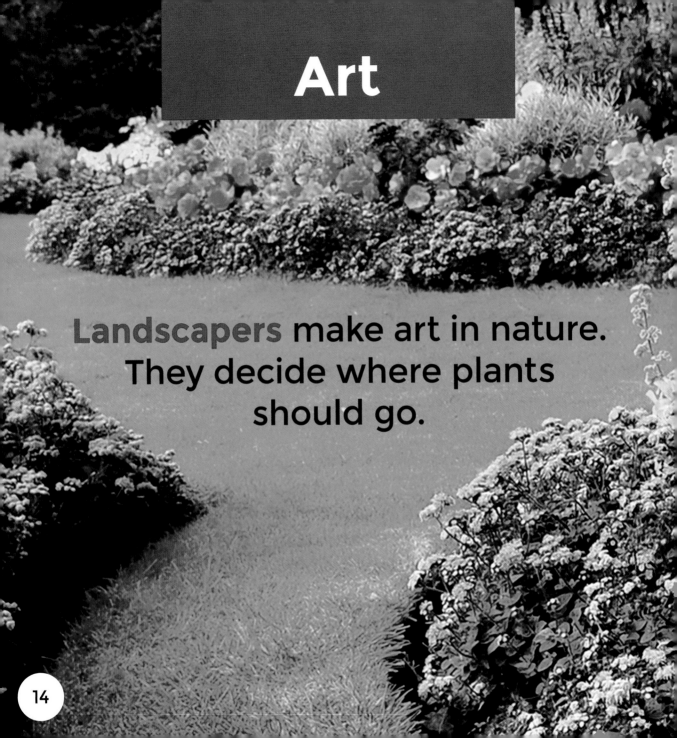

Art

Landscapers make art in nature. They decide where plants should go.

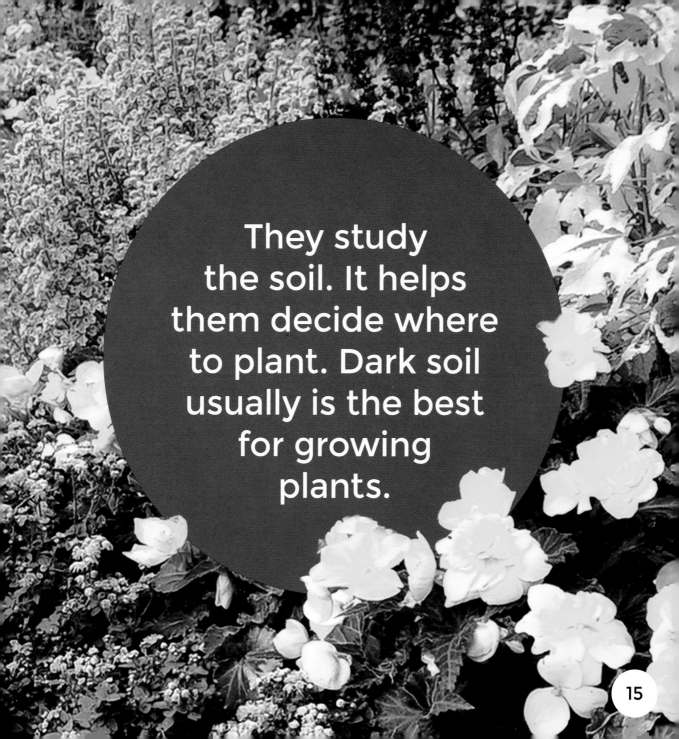

They study
the soil. It helps
them decide where
to plant. Dark soil
usually is the best
for growing
plants.

Math

The soil layer varies from place to place. It can be as shallow as 1 foot (0.3 m). Or it can be as deep as 100 feet (30 m).

Soil is full of life.

One square yard (0.8 sq. m.)
can have 100 to 500 worms!

- Some people use compost in gardens. It is made from food waste. Compost gives soil nutrients. This helps plants grow.

- Many tiny living creatures are in soil. They are called microbes. Microbes are very small. Most are too small to see. But they have important jobs. They break down dead plants and animals. This gives soil lots of nutrients.

Glossary

landscaper - one who changes the land to make it more beautiful, especially by adding plants.

mineral - a substance that forms naturally under the ground.

nutrient - an essential food that plants need to grow.

remains - what is left of the body after an animal or plant dies.

retaining wall - a structure that holds back earth.

Booklinks

For more information on soils, please visit abdobooklinks.com

Learn even more with the Abdo Zoom STEAM database. Check out abdozoom.com for more information.

Index